Journey of the BATS

BY BENJAMIN O. SAMUELSON

Gareth Stevens
PUBLISHING

Please visit our website, www.garethstevens.com. For a free color catalog of all our high-quality books, call toll free 1-800-542-2595 or fax 1-877-542-2596.

Cataloging-in-Publication Data

Names: Samuelson, Benjamin O.
Title: Journey of the bats / Benjamin O. Samuelson.
Description: New York : Gareth Stevens Publishing, 2019. | Series: Massive animal migrations | Includes index.
Identifiers: ISBN 9781538212400 (pbk.) | ISBN 9781538216712 (library bound) | ISBN 9781538216729 (6 pack)
Subjects: LCSH: Bats--Juvenile literature.
Classification: LCC QL737.C5 S26 2019 | DDC 599.4--dc23

First Edition

Published in 2019 by
Gareth Stevens Publishing
111 East 14th Street, Suite 349
New York, NY 10003

Copyright © 2019 Gareth Stevens Publishing

Designer: Katelyn E. Reynolds
Editor: Joan Stoltman

Photo credits: Cover, pp. 1, 19 Nick Garbutt/Barcroft Media/Getty Images; cover, pp. 1–24 (background) Vadim Georgiev/Shutterstock.com; cover, pp. 1–24 (background) CS Stock/Shutterstock.com; p. 5 Samart Sing/Shutterstock.com; p. 7 Kirsanov Valeriy Vladimirovich/Shutterstock.com; p. 9 Jurgen Freund/naturepl.com/Nature Picture Library/Getty Images; p. 11 KKulikov/Shutterstock.com; p. 13 satit_srihin/Shutterstock.com; p. 15 Philip Dalton/Nature Picture Library/Getty Images; p. 17 (map) Serban Bogdan/Shutterstock.com; p. 17 (bat) Michael Durham/Minden Pictures/Getty Images; p. 21 Blue Planet Studio/Shutterstock.com.

Printed in the United States of America

CPSIA compliance information: Batch #CS18GS: For further information contact Gareth Stevens, New York, New York at 1-800-542-2595.

CONTENTS

WORDS IN THE GLOSSARY APPEAR IN **BOLD** TYPE THE FIRST TIME THEY ARE USED IN THE TEXT.

So Many Kinds OF BATS

Earth has more than 1,300 species, or kinds, of bats! Some are large and live in hot, wet forests, eating fruit. Others are tiny and suck nectar from flowering desert plants. Some even live in the woods, eating bugs.

Many foods only show up at certain times of the year. What's a bat to do? Bats can **hibernate** until food returns. They can also migrate and then hibernate until food returns. Or they can migrate to a new food supply!

> ### THERES MORE!
> BATS THAT EAT FOODS LIKE FRUIT OR NECTAR TIME THEIR MIGRATION SO THEY ARRIVE WHEN FOOD IS IN SEASON. BUG-EATING BATS KNOW JUST WHEN TO ARRIVE, TOO!

Migration is when a group of animals moves every year around the same time based on seasons. Only about 3 percent of bat species migrate.

5

What are Bats, ANYWAY?

Bats are the only mammals that fly! As mammals, they give birth to live young, called pups, and drink milk from the mother's body when young. They also have fur like other mammals.

Bats are mostly nocturnal, meaning they're active at night. They have great hearing, especially the species that hunt and eat bugs! Some species live in groups, called colonies, while others keep to themselves except during migration and hibernation. Some roost, or live, in trees, while others live in dark, quiet, hidden spaces.

> ## THERE'S MORE!
>
> SPEAKING OF BAT FUR, SCIENTISTS RECENTLY DISCOVERED THEY CAN LEARN HOW FAR A BAT HAS MIGRATED BY STUDYING ITS FUR! COOL!

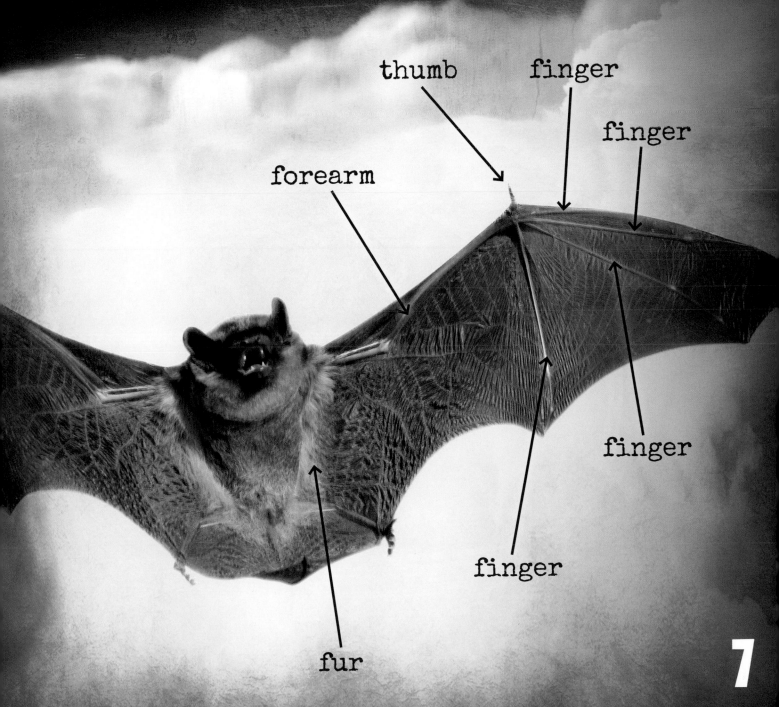

Bats fly by moving their long fingers, while birds move their forearms to fly.

thumb

finger

finger

forearm

finger

finger

fur

7

Bat BABIES

Some species of bats **mate** at the end of summer, when females have just eaten many **nutrients**. In some bat species, males and females have different migrations because females need to get to a place with good food.

Some females even migrate while **pregnant**! Sometimes, it's because her body needs the nutrients while she's pregnant. Other times, it's to make sure her newborn pup has good food once it's born. Bat pups are often born in spring, when there are plenty of flowers, nectar, and bugs!

THERE'S MORE!

BATS NEED LOTS OF **ENERGY** TO GROW, FLY, AND MIGRATE! THEY OFTEN EAT THEIR WEIGHT IN FOOD EVERY NIGHT DURING FEEDING SEASON TO COLLECT AS MUCH ENERGY AS THEY CAN.

After eating, bats sleep upside down. While they sleep, their bodies take nutrients from their food and store the nutrients in fat. Then, they turn over and poop out everything else so they're light enough to fly!

bat pup

why HIBERNATE?

Some bats save energy for their spring migration by hibernating in their winter home! While hibernating, they enter a state called torpor. In torpor, they save energy by slowing their heartbeats and breathing and lowering their body **temperature.** In torpor, bats can even go minutes without taking a breath!

Their hibernaculum (hy-buhr-NAA-kyuh-luhm), or the place where they hibernate, must be quiet and have an even temperature. Being woken from torpor uses up much-needed migration, flying, and hunting energy!

> **THERE'S MORE!**
>
> A BAT'S HEART NORMALLY BEATS 300 TO 400 TIMES PER MINUTE. IN TORPOR, IT CAN BEAT AS FEW AS 10 TIMES A MINUTE!

How'd They DO THAT?

A few species of bats have migrations over 1,000 miles (1,609 km), which are some of the longest animal migrations in the world! Bats lose 0.02 ounce (0.5 g) of stored fat for every 62 miles (100 km) they fly!

Flying long distances means bats have to know where they're going, otherwise they'll run out of energy. Bats have special matter in their cells that can tell direction just like a magnet in a **compass**! Cool!

> ## THERE'S MORE!
>
> BATS ARE ALSO THE ONLY MAMMAL THAT KNOWS WHAT DIRECTION THEY'RE FACING BASED ON THE LIGHT DURING SUNSETS.

Bats have special parts in their eyes that can see light in the sunset in a way that people's eyes can't!

13

To the BAT CAVE!

Bracken Cave in Texas is home to the largest bat colony—and the largest mammal group—on Earth! Over 10 million female Mexican free-tailed bats give birth and raise their young there in summer.

These bats migrate up to 1,000 miles (1,609 km) from Mexico to Texas, flying up to 60 miles (97 km) an hour if the wind is with them! They give birth soon after arriving. The population doubles after the females give birth, so 20 million bats spend the summer eating a high-fat diet of moths.

>THERE'S MORE!<

BECAUSE MEXICAN FREE-TAILED BATS LIVE IN MUCH OF SOUTHWESTERN NORTH AMERICA, COLONIES WORK IN SEVERAL DIFFERENT WAYS. SOME MIGRATE, BUT DON'T HIBERNATE. OTHERS DON'T MIGRATE, BUT DO HIBERNATE. SOME DON'T MIGRATE OR HIBERNATE!

At Bracken Cave, 20 million bats fly out of one cave opening. Many people come to watch the bats fly out, an event that lasts 3 hours!

15

The Longest Migration in
MAMMAL HISTORY

Around 10,000 years ago, a pregnant hoary bat—or maybe a small group of hoary bats including males and females—flew nonstop from somewhere in North America to the Hawaiian Islands. They've since **developed** a very unusual migration pattern.

The hoary bats in North America migrate in fall from the cold north to the warm south. That makes sense, right? But Hawaiian hoary bats move to colder areas in the winter! They travel north and up into the mountains of Hawaii!

> **THERE'S MORE!**
>
> THE RAINFORESTS WHERE THE HAWAIIAN HOARY BATS LIVE IN SUMMER HAVE HEAVY RAINS IN WINTER THAT MAKE IT HARD TO FIND BUGS TO EAT. THEY MOVE NORTH BECAUSE IT'S DRIER!

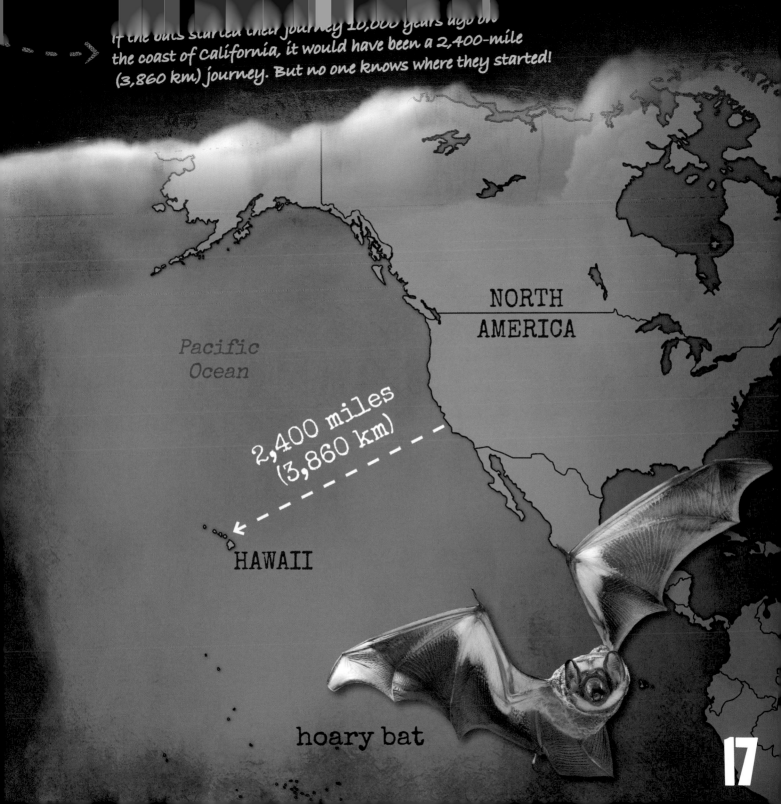

If the bats started their journey 10,000 years ago on the coast of California, it would have been a 2,400-mile (3,860 km) journey. But no one knows where they started!

NORTH
AMERICA

Pacific
Ocean

2,400 miles
(3,860 km)

HAWAII

hoary bat

17

A Blizzard OF BATS

The largest mammal migration on Earth is in Africa, but it isn't zebras or wildebeests. It's the straw-colored fruit bat migration!

Over 8 million straw-colored fruit bats migrate to Kasanka National Park in Zambia late every October to eat fruit. They strip trees bare and then disappear at the end of December. No one knows where they live the rest of the year! Tracking has shown that they live at least 620 miles (1,000 km) away, but it could be double that!

THERE'S MORE!

THE FEMALE STRAW-COLORED FRUIT BATS MIGRATE TO ZAMBIA WHILE VERY PREGNANT. PREGNANCY AND MIGRATION BOTH USE A LOT OF ENERGY, SO THE NUTRIENTS IN THESE FRUITS MUST BE REALLY IMPORTANT!

Over 1 billion pieces of fruit are eaten from just a 2.5-acre (1 ha) part of Zambia. These bats eat twice their weight in fruit every night and then rest in trees during the day.

A Changing WORLD

Climate change is a serious danger to bats. It can affect when—and even where—fruits, bugs, and nectar can be found. If bat migrations don't happen at the same time food is ready, bats won't have enough energy to survive and will die off.

Wind turbines—which create electricity using wind—are often placed in the migration path of bats, killing hundreds of thousands of bats yearly. Hopefully, power companies will study bat migrations and find safer places to put wind turbines!

THERE'S MORE!

WHITE-NOSE SYNDROME IS CAUSED BY A KIND OF FUNGUS THAT KILLS 1 MILLION BATS A YEAR. THE FUNGUS WAKES THEM FROM HIBERNATION, WASTING THEIR ENERGY.

Bats are mostly killed by wind turbines during their fall migration south. Bat deaths can drop almost 75 percent if turbines are turned off during low wind nights in fall. But will power companies turn off their turbines to save bats?

21

GLOSSARY

climate change: long-term change in Earth's climate, caused partly by human activities such as burning oil and natural gas

compass: a tool for finding directions that uses a magnetic needle

develop: to grow and change

energy: power to do work

fungus: a living thing that is somewhat like a plant, but doesn't make its own food, have leaves, or have a green color

hibernate: to be in a sleeplike state for an extended period of time, usually during winter

mate: to come together to make babies

nutrient: something a living thing needs to grow and stay alive

pregnant: carrying an unborn baby in the body

temperature: how hot or cold something is

turbine: a motor operated by the movement of water, steam, or air

FOR MORE INFORMATION

Books

Berman, Ruth. *Let's Look at Bats*. Minneapolis, MN: Lerner, 2010.

Gray, Susan H. *Bats Sleep Upside Down*. Ann Arbor, MI: Cherry Lake Publishing, 2016.

Hibbert, Clare. *Bat Hospital*. New York, NY: PowerKids Press, 2015.

Websites

Amazing Bats of Bracken Cave
kids.nationalgeographic.com/explore/nature/amazing-bats-of-bracken-cave/#bracken-cave.jpg
Read all about the 20 million bats that live at Bracken Cave in Texas.

Bat Cams
batconservation.org/discover/bat-cams/
Cameras inside a bat house let you watch fruit bats or vampire bats whenever you want!

Gardening for Bats
bats.org.uk/pages/encouraging_bats.html
Read these tips on how you can make your yard more bat friendly!

INDEX